Young
Abraham Lincoln

Log-Cabin President

A Troll First-Start® Biography

by Andrew Woods
illustrated by Pat Schories

Troll Associates

Library of Congress Cataloging-in-Publication Data

Woods, Andrew.
  Young Abraham Lincoln, log-cabin president / by Andrew Woods;
illustrated by Pat Schories.
      p.   cm.—(First-start biographies)
  Summary: A simple biography of the man who was president of the
United States during the Civil War.
    ISBN 0-8167-2532-2 (lib. bdg.)   ISBN 0-8167-2533-0 (pbk.)
    1. Lincoln, Abraham, 1809-1865—Juvenile literature.
2. Presidents—United States—Biography—Juvenile literature.
[1. Lincoln, Abraham, 1809-1865. 2. Presidents.] I. Schories,
Pat, ill. II. Title.
E457.905W66 1992
973.7′092—dc20
  [B]   91-26570

Abraham Lincoln was the sixteenth president of the United States.

Lincoln did not start his life being rich
or powerful. He was born in a log cabin
in Kentucky on February 12, 1809.

Abe had an older sister named Sarah.
Abe and Sarah and their parents had
a farm in the woods.

Life in the wilderness was hard.
There were many chores to do.
Abe fetched water from the creek,
chopped firewood, and helped his
father plant seeds.

Several miles from the Lincoln home
was a one-room schoolhouse. Abe was
very smart and he loved school. But
there was so much work to do on the
farm that Abe and Sarah went to
school for less than a year.

Abe kept learning even though he
could not go to school. He studied
at night by the light of the fire.

When Abe was 7, his family moved
to Indiana.

It was winter when the Lincolns
arrived in Indiana. Young Abe helped
his father chop down trees and build
a snug cabin.

12

Abe was only 9 when his mother got sick and died. The cabin was very lonely without her.

A year later, Abe's father got married
again. Abe's stepmother was named
Sarah Johnston. She had 3 children
of her own. Soon the log cabin was
a cheerful place again.

Abe liked to joke with his stepmother.
One day he brought a small boy with
muddy feet into the cabin...and walked
him up the wall and across the ceiling.

When Mrs. Lincoln saw the footprints,
she laughed and wondered how this
could happen.

As he grew up, Abe never lost his love of learning. He read whenever he could. He even read while he was plowing his father's fields!

Books were hard to get in the
wilderness. Sometimes Abe
walked miles to borrow one.

Once Abe borrowed a book and got it wet. He worked for 3 days to pay for the damage.

Abe grew up to be tall and strong.
He could chop wood faster than
anyone. He earned money by
splitting logs for fences.

Abe was also a great storyteller.
People loved to sit and listen to
his funny tales.

When Abe grew up, he tried many different jobs. He worked as a farmer and a carpenter. He worked on river boats and in a sawmill, too.

Then Abe opened a store. One day a
man came in with an old barrel to sell.
Abe didn't know it, but that barrel
would change his life.

Abe bought the barrel. In it he found
a book about law. Abe read it every
chance he could.

Now Abe knew what he wanted to do.
He would become a lawyer and help
people.

A lawyer named John T. Stuart helped
Abe study. It was hard work, but Abe
was determined to learn.

Finally the day came when Abe was ready to practice law. Stuart made Abe his partner. Soon Abe became very successful.

But being a lawyer was not enough for
Abe. He wanted to help people in other
ways. So he held several government
offices, too.

In 1861, Abe became the 16th president of the United States.

Abraham Lincoln was president during the Civil War. This was a very sad time for the country. But Lincoln kept the nation together. Then, just as the war ended in 1865, an angry man shot and killed President Lincoln.

Thousands of people wept when they heard Lincoln was dead. Today, many people still visit his memorial in Washington, D.C.